Contents

AF605642

A material world

The important thing in science is not so much to obtain new facts as to discover new ways of thinking about them.

Sir William Bragg (1862–1942), Nobel Prize winner (Physics) in 1915

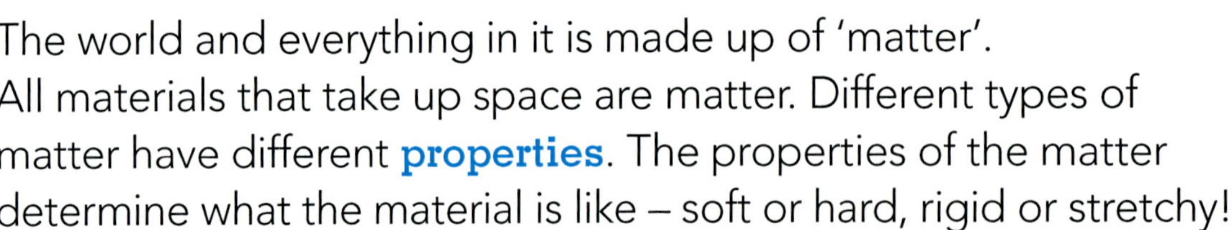

The world and everything in it is made up of 'matter'. All materials that take up space are matter. Different types of matter have different **properties**. The properties of the matter determine what the material is like – soft or hard, rigid or stretchy!

Many materials, such as wood, are very useful to us in their natural state. Other materials, though, such as coal, become much more useful to us after they are changed. We refer to materials we have changed as processed materials.

Did you know?
Sand has been useful to humans since ancient times. The Greeks and Romans used sand to filter their water.

LET'S FIND OUT

- How do we obtain materials?
- How does the removal of materials from the Earth affect the **environment**?
- What properties make materials useful?
- How can we change materials?
- What can we make by mixing different materials together?

properties special qualities or features
environment surroundings

A sculpture in Taiwan made from plastic waste to promote environmental awareness

Mining – why on Earth?

Last month *Material World* **asked our readers what they thought about mining. Read on to see what Alex had to say.**

Mining is a disaster for our environment. The materials we mine may be useful to us and many people may even feel that they can't live without them; however, mining can't go on forever.

Mining is ruining our environment. Every day, mining companies drill into the Earth and tear up our land. Forests are cut down to make way for mines, and we lose the trees that help keep our air healthy and that house hundreds of wildlife species. Poisonous chemicals used in mining run into rivers, spoiling our water supply and killing marine animals. And after the mining has finished, the mined areas of land are very rarely brought back to life.

A uranium mine cut into the Earth

mining taking materials from the ground

Polluted water flowing into a contaminated river

We clearly depend on mining to provide us with a huge range of materials that we use in our everyday lives. Much of what's around us is made from mined materials – metals, such as gold, silver, copper and iron, and non-metals, such as oil, gas, coal and salt. These materials may provide us with many **conveniences** and may seem invaluable to us, but we need to think about how using them impacts our world.

We need to realise that many of the materials we rob the Earth of are **finite** resources. This means that if we use them all up, one day they will run out.

Think about plastic shopping bags. Most are used once and then thrown away. Plastic is made from **crude** oil, which is taken out of the ground at an alarming rate.

conveniences things that make life easier or nicer
finite limited; have an end
crude raw, not processed

What will we do when we run out of materials? It's vital that we reduce, re-use and recycle to **conserve** mined materials and slow the rate at which we take them from the ground.

Mining companies can control their use of chemicals and find ways to mine without them. They can also attempt to repair damage they do to the environment.

We can each make a difference too! We can make better, more **sustainable** choices, particularly about the products we buy. For example, we can choose to purchase a car that runs on **eco-friendly** fuel or choose to carry our shopping in re-usable bags.

For the sake of our planet and of future generations, we need to stop mining before the Earth is spoilt forever and it has nothing left for us to take.

A young girl joins protesters calling for tougher mining restrictions, outside the New South Wales Parliament House, Sydney

conserve protect; stop the loss of
sustainable can be continued
eco-friendly something that does little or no harm to the environment

Breakaway tasks

Remembering

1 Name two metals that are mined from the Earth.

2 What form of oil is used to make plastic?

Understanding

3 Write three 'True' or 'False' questions about mining, using facts from the text.

4 Draw up a table to sort these materials into the categories of metal or non-metal: gold, coal, salt, uranium, iron, gas.

Applying

5 Make a T-chart and list any positive aspects of mining that you can think of in one column and any negative aspects in the other.

6 Write a letter to the prime minister, sharing your opinions about the negative effects of mining.

Analysing

7 Identify the language and facts from the article that are persuasive.

8 Make a checklist of things we can do to reduce our need for mined materials.

Evaluating

9 What do you think is the strongest argument made against mining in the article? Draw a picture that clearly illustrates the problem.

Creating

10 Write a persuasive script for a television advertisement encouraging the public to re-use, reduce and recycle materials.

Get slimed!

Slime is oozy, icky and gloopy. It's fun to make and even more fun to play with. Slime is made by mixing glue with a range of other ingredients. When mixed together, the ingredients look and feel different, and behave in a different way.

What you need

- mixing bowl
- 2 measuring cups or jugs
- tablespoon
- PVA glue
- food colouring
- borax (available from the laundry aisle at the supermarket)
- water
- ziplock bag or sealable container to store your slime
- smock, apron or old shirt
- rubber gloves

What you do

1 Collect your materials and put your smock and rubber gloves on.

2 Pour 1 cup of water into a bowl. Add 1 tablespoon of borax. Stir until the borax dissolves. Put this mixture aside.

3 Measure 1/2 cup of glue. Add 1/2 cup of water and 1/2 tablespoon of food colouring to the glue. Stir well.

4 Carefully pour the glue mixture into the water containing borax. Mix with your hands (while still wearing gloves) until slime forms.

5 Have fun playing with the slime. Experiment with the way the slime moves when it is stretched, bounced and squished. Store in a sealed container.

Slimy options

- **Magnetic slime:** Replace the food colouring with black pigment (available from art and craft stores). Make sure the black pigment contains iron oxide – this is what makes the slime magnetic.
- **Creepy slime:** Add plastic worms, insects or eyeballs (not real ones!) to your slime. This slime is great for Halloween!
- **Cornflour slime:** You can make slime using cornflour instead of glue. Add 1 teaspoon of food colouring to 1/2 cup of warm water. Gradually stir the water into 1 cup of cornflour. You might not need to add all the water.

Safety notes

- Do NOT eat the slime! Borax is poisonous.
- Wear rubber gloves to protect your hands.
- Wash your hands after playing with the slime.
- The slime might stain your clothes and other surfaces, so be careful how and where you play with it!

Breakaway tasks

Remembering

1 What type of glue is used to make the slime?

2 How much borax is used in the recipe?

Understanding

3 What can you learn about materials from this experiment? Record ideas on a mind-map.

4 In a table, identify two other uses for each of the ingredients used to make slime.

Applying

5 Make a flow chart to show the steps involved in making the slime. Draw an illustration for each step.

6 Write a persuasive letter to your teacher telling him/her why making slime would be a good experiment for other students to do too.

Analysing

7 What do you think would happen if you didn't add enough water to the slime mixture? What if you added too much water?

8 Use the Similar and Different graphic organiser to compare facts about the glue slime with facts about the cornflour slime.

Evaluating

9 Recommend any extra steps that you think would make the instructions in the article easier to follow.

Creating

10 Imagine you are the creator of slime, and that you are going to sell it in toyshops. Think of a catchy name for your slime and design the packaging for it.

More than just sandcastles

Have you ever had a really good look at sand? You've probably built a castle from sand, but you might not know that sand is used to make a lot of the things that we use every day.

Playing with sand at the beach

Sand is made up of thousands and thousands of tiny grains. The most common type of sand is mostly made up of silica, also known as silicon dioxide (which is a mixture of silicon and oxygen). When silica is heated to very high **temperatures** (sometimes more than 1600°C), it can change shape and form. At these temperatures, the silicon can also be separated from the oxygen. Both silica and silicon can be mixed with other materials to change the way it looks, feels and behaves. Some of the materials and products that are created by processing silica and silicon are examined below.

Glass

Silica is the main ingredient used to make glass. Items we make from glass include windows, bottles, microscope lenses and mirrors. One property of glass is that it is usually transparent (you can see through it). This makes it useful for windows. However, glass is also brittle and shatters into pieces if hit hard.

temperatures levels of heat

Optical fibres

Optical fibres are thin tubes, often made of glass, that carry information at high speeds via laser light. Optical fibres are used in Internet, telephone and pay television cables, which run underground and support many of our **communication** and entertainment **technologies**.

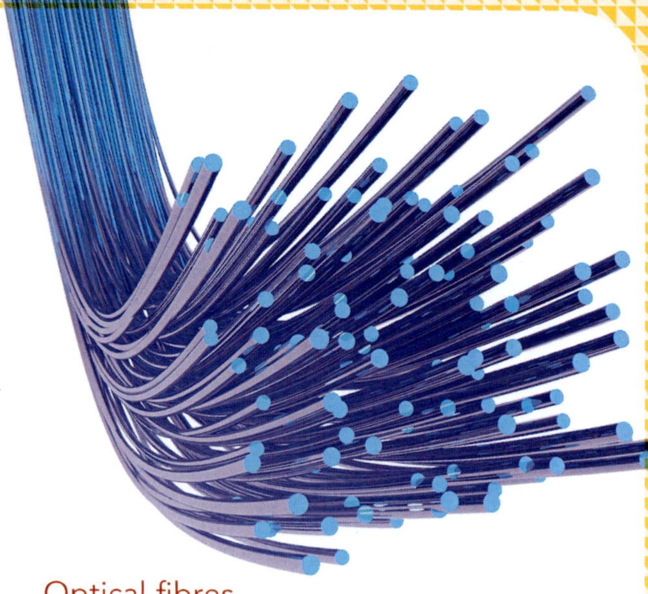

Optical fibres

Silicone

Silicon can be separated out from silica. It can then be used as the base product of silicone, which is a strong, flexible and water-resistant material. These properties make silicone a useful material to create non-stick cookware, as well as pastes and gels to fill gaps in walls and roofs.

Computer chips

Computer chips process information. They are made from small pieces of silicon. Silicon does not **conduct** electricity, so the silicon used in computer chips is mixed with other materials, such as boron, to improve this property of the material.

Solar cells

Solar cells are small pieces of silicon mixed with other materials. They store energy from the Sun, which can then be used to power our homes and electronic devices.

communication moving information between people
technologies devices that make use of scientific knowledge
conduct allow to pass through

Breakaway tasks

Remembering

1 What is the main material that sand is made of?
2 How is silica used to make different products?

Understanding

3 List items in your classroom that are made from silica.
4 Draw four squares. In each, draw an item that uses optical fibres, silicone, computer chips or solar cells.

Applying

5 Make a timeline to show the order in which you think the products in the article were invented. Research on the Internet to see if you were correct.
6 Write a catchy newspaper headline about the discovery of glass.

Analysing

7 Write a short biography of a person who discovered an important use for silica, such as Robert Noyce or Jack Kilby, who together invented the silicon computer chip.

Evaluating

8 Create an advertisement for a silica product.
9 Suggest alternative materials for making products usually made from silica.

Creating

10 Design the front cover of your very own magazine, *Silica*. Include some exciting headlines for articles in the magazine.

A very slow drip

by Joee Kelk

The tension is slowly building at the University of Queensland, as researchers eagerly await the ninth drop of the Pitch Drop Experiment to fall. The eighth drop fell back in 2000.

Started in 1927 by Professor Thomas Parnell, the Pitch Drop Experiment is one of the world's longest-running science experiments. Only two drops fell before Parnell died in 1948. This very old and famous experiment aims to show that the substance pitch, which seems solid, actually flows very slowly. At room temperature pitch is hard and shatters like glass when hit with a hammer.

Viscosity describes how quickly or slowly a substance can move. Pitch's viscosity is around 100 billion times higher than that of water, which is why the Pitch Drop Experiment only drips once every 8 to 13 years. In 84 years, no one has ever seen the pitch drop fall.

Source: *The Helix*, Issue 141 (Dec 2011–Jan 2012), 'A Very Slow Drip' by Joee Kelk, page 7

Professor John Mainstone was custodian of the Pitch Drop Experiment for 52 years.

pitch a thick, dark substance in different forms (one of which is the remains of concentrated tar or bitumen)
viscosity ability to and speed at which something can flow

Breakaway tasks

Remembering

1 What are people at the University of Queensland waiting for?

2 When did the Pitch Drop Experiment begin?

Understanding

3 Answer 'True' or 'False' to the following statements:
   - a Pitch is a fast-flowing liquid.
   - b The eighth drop of pitch fell in 1998.
   - c In 84 years, no one has seen a pitch drop fall.

4 Write a concrete poem about pitch using a range of adjectives.

Applying

5 Write a list of major world events that have happened since the last pitch drop in 2000.

6 Draw a cartoon of the pitch drop. Give it a face and expressions. What might it say to other substances, such as water, that drip much more quickly?

Analysing

7 Research on the Internet to find another substance similar to pitch. Write a short report about it.

8 Make a Venn diagram to compare the differences and similarities between pitch and another substance.

Evaluating

9 Do you think the Pitch Drop Experiment is worthwhile? Make a list of things scientists might learn from it.

Creating

10 Imagine you are being interviewed as the first person to see a pitch drop fall. List questions your interviewer might ask, and record interesting answers.

Strands in action

Core tasks

1 Imagine you are a scientist in the world's craziest toy laboratory. You have been asked to invent a new substance. Your new substance should have one exciting property. Make a labelled diagram and a PMI chart about your new substance. Then, write a radio advertisement for your substance. Make an audio recording of your advertisement and share it with the class.
2 Create a class or school plan to promote the 'reduce, re-use and recycle' message. Find a creative way to present your top five recommendations to your class.

Extra tasks

1 Make your own word-find puzzle about materials.
2 Design a house made entirely of natural materials. Label materials used.
3 Make a T-chart, listing natural materials on one side and a processed version of each on the other.
4 Make a poster encouraging other students to reduce their use of non-renewable materials at home.

A synonym is a word that has a very similar meaning to another word. Using synonyms can add colour and interest to your writing.